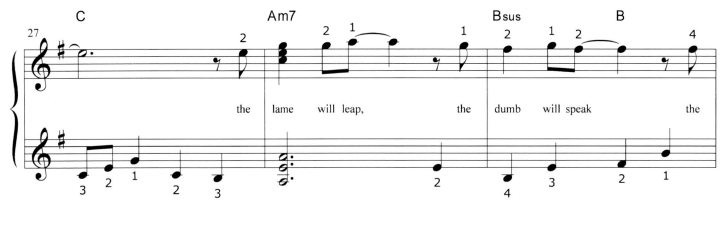

the lame will leap, the dumb will speak the

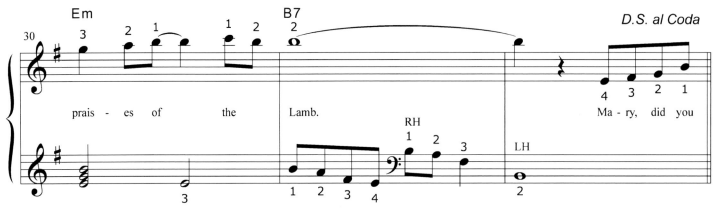

prais - es of the Lamb.

D.S. al Coda

RH
LH

Ma - ry, did you

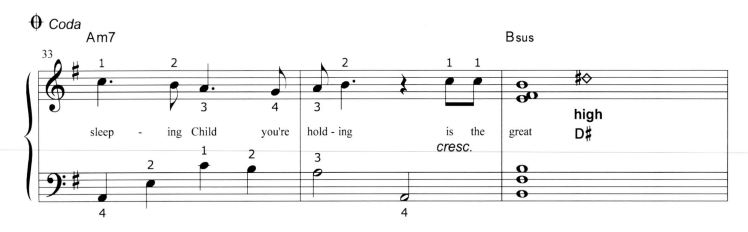

$\oplus$ *Coda*

sleep - ing Child you're hold - ing is the great

cresc.

**high
D♯**

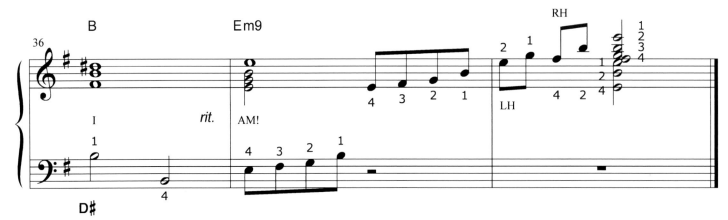

I

rit. AM!

RH
LH

D♯

3

Mary, Did You Know?
Intermediate Arrangement *(See back cover for details)*

Harp arrangement by Sylvia Woods

Words and Music by
Mark Lowry and Buddy Greene